STILL LIFE WITH LOOPS
NATURALEZA MUERTA CON LAZOS

Eli Tolaretxipi
STILL LIFE WITH LOOPS
NATURALEZA MUERTA CON LAZOS

҈

Translated by
Philip Jenkins

Introduced by Robert Crawford

2008

Published by Arc Publications,
Nanholme Mill, Shaw Wood Road
Todmorden OL14 6DA, UK

Original Spanish poems copyright © Eli Tolaretxipi 1999 & 2003
Translation copyright © Philip Jenkins 2003 & 2006
Translation copyright in 'The Fish' © Philip Jenkins
& Eli Tolaretxipi 2003
Introduction copyright © Robert Crawford 2008

Design by Tony Ward
Printed by the MPG Books Group
in the UK

978 1904614 46 3 (pbk)
978 1904614 95 1 (hbk)

ACKNOWLEDGEMENTS
Quotation from the poem 'Track' by
Tomas Tranströmer from
*The Half-Finished Heaven:
The Best Poems of Tomas Tranströmer*,
chosen and translated by Robert Bly,
Graywolf Press, Saint Paul, Minnesota, 2001

Cover photograph is by Angela Bonadies

The publishers acknowledge financial assistance from
ACE Yorkshire

Arc Publications: 'Visible Poets' series
Editor: Jean Boase-Beier

To Ekain and Joana

CONTENTS

Translator's preface / 10
Introduction / 14

from
PAST LOVE STILL LIFE

20 / I, I / 21
22 / I, II / 23
24 / I, III / 25
26 / I, IV / 27
28 / I, V / 29
30 / I, VII / 31
32 / I, VIII / 33
34 / I, XIII / 35
36 / I, XXVII / 37
38 / I, XXVIII / 39
40 / I, XXXI / 41
42 / I, XXXIV / 43
44 / I, XXXV / 45
46 / II, I / 47
48 / II, II / 49
50 / II, III / 51
52 / II, V / 53
54 / II, VI / 55
56 / II, X / 57
58 / II, XII / 59
60 / II, XIII / 61

64 / El Pez • The Fish / 65

from
THE LOOPS OF THE FIGURE

68 / Es un pasaje estrecho • There is a narrow passage / 69
70 / Yo estoy ahí • I am there / 71
72 / Cercada por una luz que desprende • The street is surrounded by a light / 73
74 / Lectura 27-XII-2000 11 pm • Reading 27-XII-2000 11 pm / 75

76 / Lectura 29-xii-2000 1.00 am	• Reading 29-xii-2000 1.00 am / 77
78 / Lectura 8-i-2001 5.45 am	• Reading 8-i-2001 5.45 am / 79
80 / Conferencia 13-i-2001 7.30 pm	• Lecture 13-i-2001 7.30 pm / 81
82 / Lectura 9	• Reading 9 / 83
84 / La máquina de museo resopla…	• The engine from the museum snorts… / 85
86 / El cuerpo del agua está metido	• The mass of water is enclosed / 87
88 / En sueños mato a uno,	• In dreams I kill someone, / 89
90 / Petirrojo de cuerpo diminuto, …	• A robin with a tiny body, … / 91
92 / Padre	• Father / 93
94 / Madre	• Mother / 95
96 / Yo	• Me / 97
98 / Me coloco detrás de él	• I stand behind him / 99
100 / Nada ocurre tal y como ocurre en el poema.	• Nothing happens in the way that it happens in the poem. / 101
102 / La noche pasa como una enfermedad…	• The night passes like an illness… / 103
104 / La cama es un pozo	• The bed is a well / 105
106 / La máquina de museo consigue detener el agua,	• The engine from the museum manages to stop the water, / 107
108 / Hay un sobresalto inesperado pero regular	• She has an unexpected but regular fright / 109
110 / El viento debe de ser eso:	• The wind must be this: / 111
112 / Paso las hojas de la libreta	• I turn the pages of the notebook / 113
114 / Me cortan un trozo de carne del hombro.	• They cut a piece of skin from my shoulder. / 115
116 / Los cuerpos se tienden sobre…	• The bodies lie down on… / 117
118 / El viento de la máquina bate	• The wind from the machine strikes / 119

Biographical notes / 121

SERIES EDITOR'S NOTE

There is a prevailing view of translated poetry, especially in England, which maintains that it should read as though it had originally been written in English. The books in the 'Visible Poets' series aim to challenge that view. They assume that the reader of poetry is by definition someone who wants to experience the strange, the unusual, the new, the foreign, someone who delights in the stretching and distortion of language which makes any poetry, translated or not, alive and distinctive. The translators of the poets in this series aim not to hide but to reveal the original, to make it visible and, in so doing, to render visible the translator's task too. The reader is invited not only to experience the unique fusion of the creative talents of poet and translator embodied in the English poems in these collections, but also to speculate on the processes of their creation and so to gain a deeper understanding and enjoyment of both original and translated poems.

Jean Boase-Beier

TRANSLATOR'S PREFACE

I first encountered the poetry of Eli Tolaretxipi in an Italian poetry magazine, where a small selection of poems from her first book was published in Spanish and Italian several years ago. I was intrigued by the physicality of the poems and by the fact that they sought to delineate difficult emotions through the language of the visual arts, rather than through a more direct description of emotional turmoil. Eli Tolaretxipi often writes through objects and is therefore arguably much closer to some British and American poetry than to some of the poetry of her own country. This is not surprising as she herself is a translator of English-language verse and has made Spanish-language versions of the poetry of Sylvia Plath and Elizabeth Bishop, among others.

I have now been a reader and translator of Eli's poetry for over five years and the moment has come for me to set down some thoughts about the problems I have encountered in translating the poems which follow this translator's preface. I have remarked the physicality of her poetry and this is accompanied by a certain hermetic quality. Both characteristics can sometimes leave the translator either seeking clarification between a number of possible meanings or reassurance that the translation reflects the original.

I have benefited from getting to know the poet and visiting her twice in San Sebastian. Her English is also of mother-tongue standard, so she has also been the most insightful of editors. To have the poet before you is, of course, a tremendous privilege and one which is not available to the translators of Quevedo, Machado or García Lorca or of many other wonderful poets who have written in Spanish. Eli Tolaretxipi has also helped me greatly with the references to other works of imaginative literature, be they poetry or fiction, which occur in her poems.

So as the more easily to be able to refer to those poems, I will briefly describe Eli's two collections and the way in which I have made my selection from them, itself a problem for an anthology of this nature. Eli's first collection, *amor muerto naturaleza muerta* (past love still life), was published in 1999. The book contains 48 poems which are divided into two sections. The first section bears the same title as the collection and consists of 35 poems which are largely concerned with the emotional difficulties resulting from the end of a relationship. The second section is entitled *Recuerdo* (Memory) and contains 13 much shorter and more brittle poems which inhabit an uncertain world of reflection and recall.

Los lazos del número (The Loops of the Figure) is Eli Tolaretxipi's second collection and was published in Spain in October 2003. This is a work of some formal complexity, consisting of 51 poems which are patterned using the number three. So there are three parts to the book. The first part consists of one section of three poems and one of nine. The second part consists of nine sets of three poems and the third part mirrors the first with one section of nine and one of three. The poems in this book create a narrative uncertainty and are concerned with the nature of poetry and perception and with the description of dreams and of photographs.

The title of the second collection is taken from Virginia Woolf's *The Waves*. The "loops" of the title are in the plural in Spanish, although the "loop" of the original English is singular. This shift into plurality reflects the number of different voices that can be heard in the work as well as the number patterning which gives it its structure.

Both collections are carefully shaped and constructed in such a way as to make the reader aware that he is reading a poetry collection rather than a number of disparate poems. It is therefore difficult for the translator to convey the overall architecture of both books in a selection. I have as a result sought to choose poems which reflect the central concerns of each book while, particularly in the case of the second collection, preserving a sense of overall continuity. Also included here is the poem 'El pez' ('The Fish'), a tribute to Marianne Moore and Elizabeth Bishop, which explicitly connects Eli Tolaretxipi to the English-language poetry which she so reveres.

And now to the words themselves. Given the physicality of the poetry, I last went to San Sebastian with a number of queries concerning Spanish words which have more than one meaning in English. So, for example, in 'I dwell on the deformed', poem I, XIII from the first collection, there is a reference to crabs which are either writhing or becoming entangled in a plastic bag. They were writhing, Eli pointed out, reflecting at one remove the difficulties of the relationship being described. Another uncertainty I had was resolved simply by walking to the beach in Gros, the area of San Sebastian where I was staying. As I looked out to sea for the first time I saw a number of divers in black wetsuits. Being somewhat disoriented I asked myself "Is this art?", thinking their presence might be part of some sort of performance. In fact, the figure of the diver does inhabit Eli's second collection and so my "black body on a tabletop" in "Nothing happens in the way that it happens in the poem" became "black body on a surfboard".

Sometimes the process of alighting on the translation of a word with which both poet and translator are comfortable resembles the line of inquiry in a detective novel. The word *cachivache* exercised me greatly. It is used in line 16 of 'Lecture 13, I, 2001 7.30 pm', the longest poem in the selection, to describe the engine in the museum and I had originally translated it as "piece of junk", which was arguably too colloquial anyway. Eli signalled her discomfort. Walking into town one day from Gros I saw the Basque spelling of the word used as the name of a shop. Thinking that this would give me my answer I went up to the window and looked into a sort of antique shop, the sort of shop that in England would be described as selling bric-à-brac. Was that the translation? Eli once again signalled her discomfort. In the end we looked the word up in a Spanish dictionary where the definition referred to an object the name of which escapes its observer. And so *cachivache* became "thingamajig" and both poet and translator were able to relax once again.

Eli Tolaretxipi's poetry refers explicitly at times to the work of other poets. Where those poets write in English it is important to retain their original language when translating from the Spanish. For example, in the second part of the first collection Eli quotes from the work of the English poet Virginia Firnberg and it is for this reason that the phrase "this to that" recurs, even when the Spanish which echoes this English phrase changes.

Sometimes knowing a poet's point of departure for writing a poem helps the translator to be more assured of his or her translation. The enigmatic poem 'Reading 9' from *The Loops of the Figure* is a case in point. Eli explained to me that the poem makes use of the psychoanalytical notion that a woman becomes an adult when she ceases to imagine her mother attached to a line. Knowing this, although the words of the translation may not change, my understanding of the poem in question is greatly increased and I can pass on this understanding here, if the reader does not already share it.

The poems of Eli's second collection also refer to other writers and the poetic voice in the penultimate line of the collection says that it is "on the shore of the books". One reference is particularly illustrative. I had been rather puzzled by the penultimate poem in the collection "The bodies lie down on...". The poem begins with a number of bodies lying down on inflated tyres which rock on water. But then that water leaks into the flat underneath. Later in the poem it is a lung which quickens the rhythm of the tide, suggesting that both the tide and the whole scenario are imaginary. This was not a poem that was difficult to translate from the point of view of vocabulary or syntax, but the meaning remained cryptic. Once again in conversation with the poet I became aware that this poem had been inspired by reading the short-story 'La casa inundada' ('The Flooded House') by the Uruguayan writer Felisberto Hernández (1902-1964), a story in which a woman inhabits a flooded house. Felisberto, whom Italo Calvino regarded as unique, was an important avant-garde novelist and short story writer who departed from the narrative conventions of his day to produce original work in which his enigmatic imagination held sway. Possessed of this knowledge I feel more comfortable with my own translation of this enigmatic poem and indeed have been made aware of another writer of great interest.

Philip Jenkins

INTRODUCTION

It was a visual image in Eli Tolaretxipi's poetry which first caught my attention when I heard her read the translations of Philip Jenkins a few years ago:

> Green insect
> on a green apple   (p. 33)

concluding the love poem which appears in the present book as 'I, VIII', this is an image at once of merging and of separateness, of deceptive camouflage and sensuous richness. It is also witty – can the insect be seen or not? Tolaretxipi's poems often contain compelling minute physical details that have the power to lodge in the reader's attention, to make contact with the reader's dream-mind 'with the serenity of an enigma / or the obstinacy of a bat' as she puts it in another poem included here. Beauties, gleams, and serrations of the physical world are lyrically insistent in her work, but the poetry is as much about the hidden as it is about the immediately apparent. Hers is writing that returns again and again to erotic relationships, union and separation, the merging and the separateness of identity.

Though some of the poems in this book may be set in San Sebastian or somewhere very like that thronging seaboard city where Basque and Spanish meet, Tolaretxipi's work is subtle and strong in its customary avoidance of specific map references. We hear occasionally of cities identified by a letter of the alphabet, but readily identifiable placenames are oddly lacking. This encourages a more concentrated attention to small sensuous details, which is one of the rewards of Eli Tolaretxipi's poetry. The images are so clearly noticed and digested that for the reader as well as the writer they seem intimately close, and can be unsettling:

> I brush the dust from my clothes.
> Only a love which is decomposing would smell like this.   (p. 29)

or

> I shake the sawdust from my shoes.
> The room smells of onion   (p. 35)

Particles of the material world cling to these poems, however hard the speaker may sometimes wish to shake them off. Smells, sights, touches, fragments are all garnered and shed in work that is also about the weight of daily routines and the mobility, excitement, pain of desire. The desire is all the more insistent for being in no way externally politicized or commodified.

These are poems which gradually constellate into bright patterns of loss, longing, and intimate experience. They 'apply ointment to the wound', as one poem puts it, and sometimes we feel the salve, sometimes the sting. It took me several readings of these grouped, looped poems before I felt I was beginning to get the measure of them. At their best they do not seem measured, plotted, but they are nonetheless full of small, precise calibrations vital to their making. Once or twice they made me think of the erotic narratives and linkages found in a sonnet sequence. If there is a postmodern knowingness here, it is also perhaps inflected by the heritage of surrealism and by the disciplines of everyday life. Repeatedly, it was clear, loaded, simple images that made an impact as I read:

> I wring out the sponge.
> I rub my eyes a lot with soap.   (p. 35)

But such details alone are not what makes these poems. Their grace lies in the way telling details are combined with stuff that in English can seem riskily abstract, but which contributes to a sensuous, flotational quality here in writing that is both attached to recognizable daily circumstances, yet also aware of pulls beyond the mundane.

> I place the white paste draining away
> in the corners of my mouth
> the clandestine litter of desire
> installed on the highest shelves:
> delay of bodies
> rigorous calls   (p. 45)

In different proportions and differently developed, I have sensed analogous 'rigorous calls' in the work of the French poet Michel Deguy, not least in his love poems, but in Tolaretxipi's work a flotational sensation in the writing is particularly appealing and effective because focused on and enacted through miniature moments, items, and the movement of often short verse lines. So, in a zone of 'no anchors' and where arms are 'soft from swimming', the poems move us *through* – not merely across – emotional depths. We can feel 'the tide's rhythm which / the lung quickens'.

With their brief lines and frequent line-breaks, the poems' form contributes to this flotational quality, a quality of constant, sometimes edgy yet unanchored movement, a flux that is resolved into a pattern, an attunement to greater rhythms:

> The wind must be this:
> a carrier of drawn up rain   (p. 111)

We sense the world afresh as a place that is aquatic as well as inhabited. We sense life as if at times it is underwater and so seems at once impossible and intensified. While they maintain a clear syntax, the lines of the poems are honed, so that, as the poem 'Me' puts it, writing grows

> with the hair and nails
> the plants
> vinelike fingers of the geraniums
> which have to be cut back each autumn   (p. 97)

What is to be honoured and valued in these poems is something that seems at times bound up with the culture they come from – a culture of warm sunlight on fruit where a green insect looks lyrically at home. This culture contrasts strongly with the one I am part of, looking out across the crisp frost and bare twigs of an early-morning, wintry Scottish garden. Yet often in the poetry (especially, perhaps, poetry in translation) what matters most is finding the necessary, unexpected gift that becomes all the more treasured because it complements and adds to what is known and loved in one's own culture. Read with care in Philip Jenkins's translations, Eli Tolaretxipi can convey to English-speaking readers in Britain and elsewhere a gift of just this kind. Here emotion, lyricism, and realised attentiveness convince us at times that Tolaretxipi does one of the things that modern lyric poetry does best: 'She continues to speak while dreaming'.

Robert Crawford

STILL LIFE WITH LOOPS
NATURALEZA MUERTA CON LAZOS

from
PAST LOVE STILL LIFE
AMOR MUERTO NATURALEZA MUERTA

I, 1

En la ciudad D
mi amiga S
me lleva a una galería de arte
en la que hay una roca
del tamaño de la cabeza de un animal mediano
que sobresale de la pared,
inclinada hacia un cuenco
del cual podría beber
si la cabeza fuera, por ejemplo,
de leona
que aburrida que de amamantar
se toma un respiro y bebe.

Nada de esto importaría
si no fuera porque mi amiga S
me ha traído a ver
unas alas que ella misma ha construido.
En el aire dibujan algo parecido a
una mariposa
que planea desde la parte alta de la sala
de espaldas al observador.
Importa el hecho de que mi amiga S
haya construido las alas para mí,
que vaya a ser yo la mariposa
que me quede un sólo día
para decirle que ya no;
que deseo
llevarme a la leona a casa
y llenarle el cuenco con leche de verdad.

I, 1

In the city of D
my friend S
takes me to an art gallery
in which there is a rock
as large as the head of a medium-sized animal
which juts out from the wall,
leaning towards a bowl
from which it could drink
if the head were, for example,
that of a lioness,
who tired of suckling
draws breath and drinks.

None of this would matter
if it were not that my friend S
has brought me to see
some wings that she herself has constructed.
There hangs in the air what looks like
a butterfly
which is suspended from the top of the room
behind the observer.
What is important is that my friend S
has constructed the wings for me,
that I should be the butterfly
that I only have one day left
to tell her otherwise;
that I want
to take the lioness home with me
and fill her bowl with real milk.

I, II

Da miedo mirarla
pintando el mismo paisaje cada mañana
como una araña
tejiendo desde el balcón
mi cabeza
sobre el horizonte de esas playas ridículas,
para no salirse, para que no me vaya
para abarcar lo que delante
tiene
que es todo en lo que cree
porque lo puede tocar.

Así le ocurre a este cuerpo
cuando el deseo despierta
del sueño de mentir en sus brazos.

Hace ya lienzos
que en la boca entretengo un presentimiento:
la miro y veo
que mi retrato y las marinas
acabarán en la carpeta de un marchante de feria
en feria; de cama
en cama
ella,
con algo que llevarse a la boca.

I, II

It is frightening to watch her
painting the same landscape every morning
like a spider
spinning my head
from the balcony
above the horizon of these ridiculous beaches,
so as not to lose control, so that I do not leave
so that she can cope with what she has
before her
which is everything she believes in
because she can touch it.

That is what happens to this body
when desire awakens
from the dream of telling lies in her arms.

For a few canvases now
I have had a feeling:
I look at her and see
that my portrait and the seascapes
will end up in the portfolio of a seaside art dealer
on holiday; from bed
to bed
she will go,
with something to put into her mouth.

I, III

Dice que me va a vaciar.
Me venda el pecho con paños blancos
empapados en pintura pastosa
y vigila desde el espejo
esa corteza que me va saliendo:
la superficie
porosa y abultada,
la piel que tomará
el ejército de mujeres
que surja de este molde
cuando yo me haya convertido
en su falta de inspiración.

Me endurezco
y me parto
si trato de escribir.

Ahora, por ejemplo, tengo
una emergencia
emocional,
y de nada me sirven
una servilleta sucia,
un cuchillo con restos de
queso.

I, III

She says she is going to make a cast of me.
She bandages my chest with white drapes
soaked in thick brushstrokes
and from the mirror watches
this shell which I am forming:
the surface
porous and bulging,
the skin which the army
of women emerging
from this mould will assume
when I have converted myself
into her lack of inspiration.

I harden
and I shatter
if I try to write.

Now, for example, I am having
an emotional
emergency,
and a dirty serviette,
a knife with cheese left on
it are of no use
to me.

I, IV

Mi vestido es de hierro y latón.
Aquí, encogida en la circunstancia
vivo
por la curiosidad de los libros
que ella va dejando abiertos
por el asco de las uvas y los tubos de crema,
perdida la cabeza por rincones que nadie barre,
para el sabor de las almejas retorcidas
bajo mi aliento de vino.
Estoy aquí,
pecho abultado, caderas curvas
y ella no sabe de Troya y su caballo
y eso la va a perder.

I, IV

My dress is made of iron and brass.
Here, retracted in circumstance
I live
for the curiosity of the books
which she keeps on leaving open
for the abomination of the grapes and the tubes of cream,
my head lost in corners that no one sweeps,
for the flavour of devious clams
beneath my viniferous breath.
I am here,
chest bulging, hips curved
and she knows nothing of Troy and its horse
and that will be her undoing.

I, v

Me despierto en un portal
en pleno centro de la ciudad vieja de B.
Trato de reparar en el hecho de que
no volveré a estar allí.
Anoto el suceso.
Me sacudo el polvo.
Sólo un amor en descomposición olería así.
Un animal muerto hace días
entre los peldaños de la escalera
de una historia como ésta
olería así.
"Así" significa olor a carne perdida
a descuido
a desperdicio.
En algún lugar del cuerpo
el paso de sus uñas, tan sucias
siempre, de pintura
de sangre seca.
Anoto mis manos.
La falda larga cubriéndole los tobillos.
Es fácil dejar de ocultar.
Desde fuera
nadie puede leer el desánimo.
Me sacudo la cal de la ropa.

I, v

I wake up in a doorway
right in the centre of the old city of B.
I try to think of the fact that
I will not return there.
I note the incident.
I brush the dust from my clothes.
Only a love which is decomposing would smell like this.
An animal dead for days
between the steps of the staircase
of a story like this
would smell this way.
"Like this" means to smell like lost flesh
carelessly
wastefully.
In some part of the body
scratches made by her nails, always
so dirty, from painting
from dried blood.
I take note of my hands.
The broad skirt which covers her ankles.
It is easy to stop hiding things.
From outside
no one can see that I am discouraged.
I brush the flakes from my clothes.

I, VII

Me sacudo el tiempo del pelo.
El deseo de comer una naranja me ocupa.
En el cuadro
la naranja es una bola de oro
y mi corazón
una botella de plástico
y burbujas
y agua.

A este lado del marco
tropiezo con incertidumbres
aunque hay cosas seguras,
cigarrillos y naranjas,
tan porosas de puro inmediatas.

A este lado de la tierra
le pido fuego
y me ofrece miedo:
el temor de volver a su obra quieta
a la vida inmóvil.

La existencia retratada que ella comprende
me reduce
a tomarlas,
a ella, a su naranja
con todo el corazón de agua;
yo que sueño
una vida de sangre.

I, vii

I brush time from my hair.
The desire to eat an orange occupies me.
In the picture
the orange is a ball of gold
and my heart
a plastic bottle
and bubbles
and water.

On this side of the frame
I stumble over uncertainties
although there are things which are safe,
cigarettes and oranges,
so porous as to be entirely to hand.

On this side of the earth
I ask her for a light
and she offers me fear:
anxiety about returning to her quiet work
to a life without motion.

The portrayed existence that she embraces
reduces me to
take them,
her, her orange
with all my heart of water;
I who dream
of a life of blood.

I, VIII

Mi amor nace
en el agua de la ciudad muerta
y a ella vuelve cada vez.
Su amor no tiene perspectivas:
ama siempre desde el mismo lugar.

Pinto las puertas
pinto las ventanas
las cierro todas:
nadie vive en la casa raída
si no es de amor.

Debo mentir para venderla
para desatar el nudo que ella
me retuerce en la garganta.
Debo mentir para volver al agua.

Verde insecto
sobre verde manzana.

I, VIII

My love is born
in the water of the dead city
and returns to it every time.
Her love has no perspectives:
she always loves from the same place.

I paint the doors
I paint the windows
I close them all:
nobody lives in the threadbare house
if it is not of love.

I have to lie to sell it
to undo the knot that she
ties in my throat.
I have to lie to return to the water.

Green insect
on a green apple.

I, XIII

Me detengo en lo deforme.
En lo poco acorde.
Me sacudo el serrín de los zapatos.
La estancia huele a cebolla
pero no veo ninguna con la que llorar.
Los cangrejos
se retuercen en su bolsa de plástico.
Lo saben.
Sueño que ella desea cebarme
que el estómago ceda
con el hígado crecido en toda su enormidad,
e imagino presencias ocultas en las paredes.
Mi voluntad tropieza
resbala en el baño cada mañana
y sufre la conmoción del agua helada.
Estrujo la esponja.
Me froto mucho los ojos con jabón.

I, xiii

I dwell on the deformed.
On what is hardly appropriate.
I shake the sawdust from my shoes.
The room smells of onion
but I cannot see one which will make me cry.
The crabs
are writhing in their plastic bag.
They know.
I dream that she wants to fatten me up
that the stomach will give way
with the liver grown to an enormous size,
and I imagine occult presences in the walls.
My will trips over
slips in the bath every morning
and suffers the shock of freezing water.
I wring out the sponge.
I rub my eyes a lot with soap.

I, XXVII

Construye una pasarela
con hilo de pescar.
El caminar frío
agarrotado
los dedos cobardes.
Pero, quién teme al vértigo,
a la transparencia del hilo
a la delgadez de los pasos
al otro hilo
que marca arrugas
alrededor de la garganta.
Tensas
las palabras.
Beso la carne que no como.
Aplico ungüento a la herida:
cuerpo rendido
capaz de matar.

I, xxvii

She constructs a footbridge
with fishing-line.
The walk cold
stiff
the toes cowardly.
But, who is afraid of vertigo,
of the transparency of the line
of the thinness of the footsteps
of the other wire
that marks lines
around the throat?
Tense
the words.
I kiss the flesh that I do not eat.
I apply ointment to the wound:
defeated body
capable of murder.

I, xxviii

Terminada la obra
ofrece sus manos
las palmas abiertas
las grietas.
Apoyada en el andamio
balbucea
salpica
trata de explicar
el registro escuálido
de la cadera.
La nuez enorme
la bóveda inalcanzable
sobre nuestras cabezas.
Come el tiempo
los restos de manzana
entre los dientes.

I, xxviii

Having finished the work
she offers her hands
the palms open
the cracks.
Supported by the scaffolding
she stammers
spatters
tries to explain
the scrawny register
of the hip.
The enormous nutshell
the implausible vault
above our heads.
Time eats
the remains of the apple
between the teeth.

I, XXXI

No estoy
pero me veo porque estuve allí.
No reflejada en sus ojos.
Mejor,
rebotada
salida
no de sus ojos,
sino de lentes tan convexos
como para que la pretensión fuera real.
Retrocedo.
Me empujan páginas,
me quedo enganchada
en la mandíbula del libro,
pegajoso aún de aceite.
Mi caligrafía sinuosa,
muy seca ahora.
Me saco
el peso del tiempo sobre el pecho.
Pero me aplasta.

I, xxxi

I am not there
but I see myself because I was there.
Not reflected in her eyes.
Rather,
ricocheting
coming
not
from her eyes,
but from lenses so convex
as if to make the wish real.
I go back.
Pages spur me on,
I remain snared
in the jaws of the book,
still sticky with oil.
My sinuous handwriting,
very dry now.
I remove
the weight of time from my chest.
But it crushes me.

I, xxxiv

La tarde me agita y anoto
la incursión plateada de la luz
entre la regadera y el pollo,
sin plumas, blanco, poroso.
La luz vegetal se apaga al fondo.
Empuño el tenedor.
Anoto su barbaridad y la carne hundida.
La mandíbula contraída que no volverá a comer.
La piel,
colgada del hueso,
no es la historia interna
de la carne
y de las cosas.

I, xxxiv

The afternoon arouses me and I note
the silver incursion of the light
between the watering can and the chicken,
without feathers, white, porous.
The vegetal light goes out in the background.
I grasp the fork.
I note its barbarity and the sunken flesh.
The contorted jaw that will not eat again.
The skin,
hanging from the bone,
is not the real story
of the flesh
and of things.

I, xxxv

Llevo en las comisuras
la pasta blanca de lo que escurre
la camada clandestina de deseos
instalados en la estantería más alta:
demora de cuerpos
llamadas rigurosas
manos vueltas hacia aquí.
Miro hacia otro lado
y no significa perder.
Crecen.
Apilo virutas
pelo el grafito del ser
para dejar el perfil
el filo, el tono
que de una palabra a otra
anuncia el camino partido
y lo de abajo.
A la espalda,
lo que no abulta.
Láminas de hielo si bajo la vista.

I, xxxv

I place the white paste draining away
in the corners of my mouth
the clandestine litter of desires
installed on the highest shelves:
delay of bodies
rigorous calls
hands turned in this direction.
I look towards the other side
and it does not mean that I lose.
They grow.
I pile up shavings
I sharpen the pencil of the loved one
in order to leave the profile
the blade, the tone
which from one word to another
announces the road taken
and the one below.
At the shoulder,
that which does not protrude.
Sheets of ice if I lower my eyes.

II, 1

Recuerdo.
Esto a eso
esta pieza a aquella
imposible atarlas en el espacio
no hay correlación posible.

La niebla se espesa
  no se difumina
  no se disipa.
La forma de un recuerdo.
En forma de recuerdo.

No es la forma de un recuerdo la pieza.
Es el contenido.
El espesor de un recuerdo. Niebla espesa.
Recuerda.
Como trenes a través del paisaje.
No es nítido. No es claro.

II, 1

Memory.
This to that
this piece to that
impossible to connect them in space
no correlation is possible.

The fog thickens
    it does not fade
    it does not clear.
The form of a memory.
In the form of a memory.

The piece is not the form of a memory.
It is the content.
The thickness of a memory. Thick fog.
Remember.
Like trains across the countryside.
It is not vivid. It is not clear.

II, ii

Zumbido.
¿Es eco un recuerdo?
Rebota entre líneas.
No es cadencia.
No es blando el recuerdo.
Es tenso y cortante.
No. Tampoco contenedores de recuerdo lo que llega.
Hay movimiento.
Recuerdo cables.
Telegrama.
Aviso.

II, ii

Buzzing.
Is echo a memory?
It ricochets between lines.
It is not a cadence.
The memory is not soft.
It is taut and sharp.
No. Nor are containers of memory what comes.
There is movement.
I remember cables.
Telegram.
Warning.

II, III

Recuerdo.
Dos piezas.
Ésta a aquélla.
Contenidos desformatizados.
Puro transportar, como raíles, como guías.
Y cómo que es espeso el recuerdo.
Una nube.
Niebla.
Brotes de humo.

¿Es el tren el recuerdo
o su transcurrir?
¿Es el cable el recuerdo?

II, III

Memory.
Two pieces.
This to that.
Contents unformatted.
Pure transportation, like rails, like guides.
And how thick is the memory.
A cloud.
Fog.
Wisps of smoke.

Is the train the memory
or its passing by?
Is the cable the memory?

II, v

Lo electrocutamos
y llega delgado y limpio. Casi de cristal.
Cristal opaco el recuerdo.
De aristas discontinuas.
Recuerdo.
Superpuestas.
Alguna gota de sangre habrá en la memoria
si ha dejado de ser transparente
de recuerdo.
Esta pieza a aquélla
ésta a aquélla
recuerda.
Recuerdo.

II, v

We electrocute it
and it emerges slender and clean. As if glass.
Opaque glass the memory.
With broken edges.
Memory.
The edges superimposed.
There will be a drop of blood in the memory
if it has ceased to be transparent
as a keepsake.
This piece to that
this recalls
that.
Memory.

II, vi

Que alguien nos dijo adiós
y una gota de sangre
en la arista maestra del prisma.
Recuerdo.
Del raíl se desliza
de recuerdo.
Ésta a aquélla.
Una ranura
una leve laceración
rasgada la tela del presente.
Y es tijeras.

II, vi

That someone said goodbye to us
and a drop of blood
on the cutting edge of the prism.
Memory.
From the rail memory
slipped gently.
This to that.
A groove
a slight laceration
the fabric of the present torn.
And it is scissors.

II, x

Entre líneas
el rumor.
Nunca el océano tan ancho
como sus hombros.

II, x

The murmur
between lines.
Never was the ocean as broad
as her shoulders.

II, xii

¿Recuerdas?
Es otra.
Pegado el tiempo al oído.
Ahogado, detrás
lo que queda roto.
Recién venida:
mal
menos.
Aristas:
todo lo que abarca
acabado en punta.

II, xii

Do you remember?
She is different.
Time pressed against the ear.
Drowned out, behind
what remains broken.
She came recently:
it was bad
less than expected.
Edges:
everything possible
finished pointedly.

II, XIII

El recuerdo
la alarma
el aviso
sirven.
Lo que otras dijeron
despeja.
Empuja el tiempo los tímpanos.
Desata el recuerdo.
Cae más agua al agua.
No hay anclas
si el tiempo se pega al oído.

II, xiii

The memory
the alarm
the warning
have their uses.
What other women said
clears.
Time pushes on the ear drums.
Sparks the memory.
More water falls to water.
There are no anchors
if time presses on the ear.

THE FISH
EL PEZ

EL PEZ
para Marie-H Desestré

La ballena se desplaza por la superficie del agua
como una plataforma suelta
como una catedral a la deriva.
No tiene cara de cetáceo
es más bien una morena de aquarium hinchada
y afectada de prognatismo,
una gárgola derivada del futuro régimen de derribos.
Por la desembocadura del río
arrastra su enorme incomprensión
con la serenidad de un enigma
o la terquedad de un murciélago.
De ahí las grietas de su carne
y las tiras de piel que cuelgan de sus costados,
de ahí su temporal soledad, su soledad apática.
Es el sueño de una noche
impuesto por la raspa de un poema
como un arañazo de cuya causa no hay recuerdo,
y de un paseo que nunca se llevó a cabo
salvo alrededor de la ballena,
atracción que se sumerge y emerge del
agua de una bahía recortada
y pegada sobre un papel, rodeada
de los escombros de una conversación
que no llegó a cometerse del todo.

THE FISH
for Marie-H Desestré

The whale glides on the water's surface
like a loose platform
like a cathedral adrift.
It does not have the face of a cetacean
it is more like a swollen moray eel
with a projecting lower jaw,
a gargoyle derived from the future demolition regime.
Through the river's mouth
it draws its enormous lack of understanding
with the serenity of an enigma
or the obstinacy of a bat.
Hence the cracks in its flesh
and the strips of skin hanging from its sides,
hence its temporary solitude, its apathetic solitude.
It is the dream of a night
imposed by the fishbone of a poem
like the mark of a scratch the origin of which we forget,
and of a walk we never took
except around the whale,
an attraction diving and emerging
from the waters of a bay, cut out
and pasted on a piece of paper, surrounded
by the rubble of a conversation
which remained incomplete.

from THE LOOPS OF THE FIGURE
LOS LAZOS DEL NÚMERO

* * *
para Angela Bonadies

Es un pasaje estrecho
entre dos ojos
una franja poblada
de árboles altísimos
y copas con monos asomados.
Chupo mi dedo
y lo paso por ahí,
entre los ojos semicerrados.
Luego beso la boca,
que en sueños ha dicho "tres".

***
for Angela Bonadies

There is a narrow passage
between two eyes
a strip filled
with very high trees
with monkeys hanging from the treetops.
I suck my finger
and run it along there,
between the half-closed eyes.
Then I kiss the mouth,
that in dreams has said "three".

* * *

Yo estoy ahí
cuando en sueños dice
tres y despierta.
También cuando vuelve a quedarse dormida.
Cuando me muestra las fotos:
la de su madre; la de su padre delante
de una máquina de museo.
Detrás de las palmeras
ella habita ya dentro de la mujer alta.
En las ramas, en las hojas lisas.
Quién sabe si la busco
mientras camino por el borde
en sentido contrario
en el sentido contrario del desconocimiento.

* * *

I am there
when in her sleep she says
three and wakes up.
And when she falls asleep again.
When she shows me the photos:
the one of her mother; the one of her father in front
of an engine from the museum.
Behind the palm trees
she already lives inside the tall woman.
In the branches, in the smooth leaves.
Who knows if I will seek her
while I walk at the edge
in the opposite direction
in the opposite direction of ignorance.

* * *

Cercada por una luz que desprende
está la calle.
Están sus piernas
sobre unos zapatos negros de piel:
son italianos, dice.
Dos gatos, y luego otro, tres.
Cuál será la clave:
escribir como en *la Biblia de los sueños*.
Registrar.
Ver hacia dentro.
Ser inocente.
Sus palabras y sus gestos lo son.
El poema no.
En el poema todo se detiene
y es parco.
Ni siquiera analiza.
Vive. Y en él,
un discurso roto.
El tres – bello –
indescifrable.

* * *

The street is surrounded by a light
that detaches.
Her legs rise up
from black leather shoes:
they are Italian, she says.
Two cats, and then another, three.
What will be the key:
to write as in *the Bible of dreams*.
To record.
To look inwards.
To be innocent.
Her words and her gestures are.
The poem is not.
In the poem everything stops
and is meagre.
It does not even analyse.
It lives. And in it,
a broken speech.
The three – beautiful –
indecipherable.

LECTURA 27-XII-2000 11 PM

He nadado toda la noche
vestida con el traje de las lecturas
por un río sucísimo de
aguas irisadas y espuma.
Mantengo la cabeza erguida
para no tragar
las partículas flotantes
que fluyen hacia mi boca.
Respiro el poco oxígeno que
queda en el aire
y atiendo a su voz,
la voz adormecida
que adopta el tono cascado de la mujer
que fuma en el autobús
y conversa con un desconocido.

READING 27-XII-2000 11 PM

I have swum all night
dressed in the costume of the readings
through a very dirty river with
iridescent waters and foam.
I keep my head upright
in order not to swallow
the floating objects
drifting towards my mouth.
I breathe in the little oxygen which
is left in the air
and I listen to her voice,
the drowsy voice
which adopts the hoarse tone of the woman
who smokes on the bus
and is talking to a stranger.

LECTURA 29-xii-2000 1.00 am

El cuchillo,
demasiado afilado
amenaza
desde su posición en una esquina
a la mano, que,
blanca y descuidada
se araña en el aire.
Los dedos son largos y huesudos,
independientes, tanto
que jamás aprenderán nada al piano.
El vello les crece durante la noche
y después de rendido el cuerpo.

El amanecer borra la herida
y absorbe la sombra de los pelos.

Con toda naturalidad lee
y los fonemas y el aire me baten
las aletas de la nariz.
Cuenta que
hay una mujer en un autobús,
una mujer en un hospital
y un hombre que toma notas en una libreta.

READING 29-XII-2000 1.00 AM

The knife,
which is too sharp,
from its position in the corner
threatens
the hand, which,
white and neglected
is scratched in mid-air.
The fingers are broad and bony,
independent; so much so
that they will never learn to play anything on the piano.
Down grows on them during the night
and afterwards the body is exhausted.

The dawn erases the wound
and absorbs the shadow of the hairs.

She reads naturally
and the phonemes and the air strike
my nostrils.
It says that
there is a woman on a bus,
a woman in a hospital
and a man who is taking notes in a notebook.

LECTURA 8-1-2001 5.45 AM

La doctora me examina la garganta
y su saliente en forma de pico:
"todas las iglesias tienen campanario
y tú eres la cavidad abierta; a pesar
de la punta, no tienes defensas.
Tu campanita parece un plumín".
Soñaba que la muerte era un esqueleto
hecho con papel de pentagrama,
con la guadaña blanda, muy mal
recortada, y por la narración supe que
a él le había alcanzado en el pecho.
Yo seguía golpeando con mi pico agudo y preciso
y las losas saltaban en pedazos.
De la excavación salía cuarteada,
pero entera.
Al despertar me olisqueo la ropa
en busca de un indicio.
Se cierran los grifos de la noche
y el paisaje huye.
En el bolsillo
el calor de su mano, el trozo de papel,
la dirección, varios unos con forma de banderita,
un tres abultado.

READING 8-1-2001 5.45 AM

The doctor is examining my throat
and the swelling there shaped like a pickaxe:
"every church has a belfry
and you have an empty cave; in spite
of the tip, you have no defences.
Your uvula is like a nib".
I was dreaming that death was a skeleton
made from music-paper,
with a soft scythe, very badly
cut out, and from the story I knew that
he had been struck in the chest.
I continued to work with my sharp and accurate pickaxe
and the tombstones came out in pieces.
I emerged shattered from the excavation,
but whole.
When I wake up I sniff my clothes
in search of a sign.
The nocturnal taps are turned off
and the landscape disappears.
In my pocket
the heat of her hand, the scrap of paper,
the address, several ones shaped like flags,
a swollen three.

CONFERENCIA 13-I-2001 7.30 PM

Se duerme antes de apagar la luz.
No me muevo. Cierro los ojos.
Los gatos se acomodan. Son tres.
No atiendo a la numerología ni a la superstición,
aunque recuerdo que dijo tres y despertó.
Trato, más que de comprender,
de explicar. Los gatos son: rayas, movimiento,
estrabismo. Narro, cuento, explico.
Usted, discurra, comprenda, entienda lo que pueda. El poema
no es una guía práctica para ser infeliz,
ni un espejo donde usted se vea reflejado.
Tampoco es mi confesión íntima, y, cuando digo yo,
quizá no quiera decir yo. Tampoco cuando digo ella.
La máquina de museo a la que me refería es
el museo en sí, su engranaje. También es una
máquina – artefacto, cachivache –
expuesta en un museo:
el recinto que pretende contener el mundo.
Pero dije que el padre de ella se fotografió
delante de una máquina de museo y usted
me pregunta por qué. Me pregunta si me
interesa más el padre o la máquina, si el poema
es el museo.
Trato de responder. Tomo un trago
de una copita de color ámbar, redonda, chata,
singular, porque su curva es rayada y ella me la regaló
en diciembre de 2000. Fumo. La máquina
estaba ahí, era un motivo bello, y él se puso delante.
Nada más. A él le atraían el movimiento,
el chirriar de las cadenas, el olor a lubricante.
Por lo demás, era un buen médico, y no soportaba
una copa vacía. Me sirvo otro trago
con la convicción de que usted
jamás comprenderá lo que es la metáfora
y nunca aprendió a montar en bicicleta.
Sepa que en el museo, en la biblioteca
está gran parte de la sabiduría humana.
La luz sigue encendida. Beso el pelo, la nuca.
Palpo las sienes. En sueños sigue hablando.

LECTURE 13-I-2001 7.30 PM

She falls asleep before turning off the light.
I do not move. I close my eyes.
The cats make themselves comfortable. They are three.
I pay no attention to numerology or superstition,
although I recall that she said three and awoke.
I try, more than to understand,
to explain. The cats are: lines, movement,
strabismus. I narrate, I tell, I explain.
You, reflect, comprehend, understand what you can. The poem
is not a practical guide for being unhappy,
nor a mirror in which you see yourself reflected.
Neither is it my intimate confession, and, when I say I,
perhaps I do not want it to mean me. Nor when I say her.
The engine from the museum to which I refer is
the museum itself, its mechanism. It is also a
machine – artefact, thingamajig –
exhibited in a museum:
the space which claims to contain the world.
But I said that her father was photographed
in front of an engine from the museum and you
ask me why. You ask me if I
am more interested in the father or the engine, if the poem
is the museum.
I try to respond. I take a sip
from a small amber-coloured glass, round, short,
peculiar, because it has ridges and she gave it to me
in December 2000. I smoke. The engine
was there, it was an attractive subject, and he stood in front of it.
Nothing more. He was attracted by the movement,
the whirring of the chains, the smell of lubricant.
Otherwise, he was a good doctor, and could not tolerate
an empty glass. I pour myself another drop
convinced that you
will never understand what the metaphor is
and never learned to ride a bicycle.
Know that in the museum, in the library
there is a large part of human knowledge.
The light is still on. I kiss her hair, the nape of her neck.
I touch her temples. She continues to speak while dreaming.

LECTURA 9
Para Sara Zanghì

La luz sigue encendida. Cuando penetro en el sueño
hay una niña que sostiene una caña; de ella
cuelga un hilo, al cabo del cual están el aire y más abajo,
la hierba. La madre es la madeja
que rueda por el suelo y sale, con la cabeza
ocupada en sus asuntos.
La niña tira del hilo. El aire es flojo.
No hay tensión. Pronuncia las erres como en francés
y evita las eses. Ninguna hace falta para llamar a mamá.
Retoma la lectura. Tendida
miro sus dientes duros. Se mueven
como monos blancos recién despertados
en los pulmones. Cáscaras húmedas,
reventadas, como su voz al suspenderse.
La página está llena de signos
digeribles, pero alguien tiene que empujar
la sucesión, completar
los momentos.

READING 9
For Sara Zanghì

The light is still on. When I penetrate into the dream
there is a girl who is holding a rod; from it
is hanging a line, at the end of which are the air and further down,
the grass. Her mother is the skein
which rolls on the ground and leaves, bound up
in her daily tasks.
The girl draws on the line. The air is slack.
There is no tension. She pronounces her r's as in French
and avoids s's. Neither are needed to call to her mother.
She resumes reading. Lying down
I look at her hard teeth. They move
like white monkeys which have recently awoken
in her lungs. Moist shells,
shattered, like her voice when it stops.
The page is full of digestible
signs, but someone has to force
the succession, complete
the moments.

* * *

La máquina de museo resopla a punto de pararse
pero no se detiene. Sólo está el hombre, delante
de la máquina verde, y ellos, en algún lugar
del museo que queda detrás
como una turbina vibrante
dentro de la piedra que recoge el rumor de los pasos antiguos
y el calor de la materia viva de cuadros y esculturas.
El mar, motor de las aspas
se enreda en la viscosidad del hilo del río.
Es el mismo lugar visitado
por personas distintas en épocas diferentes.
La localización del lugar es imprecisa.
Tal vez sea un punto entre éste y este otro,
o tal vez esté un poco más al sur.

* * *

The engine from the museum snorts on the point of halting
but does not stop. The man stands alone, in front
of the green engine, and the others stand somewhere
in the museum which remains in the background
like a vibrating turbine
inside the stone walls which store the sound of ancient footsteps
and the heat of the living material of paintings and sculptures.
The sea, which drives the blades
gets mixed up in the viscosity of the river's trickle.
The same place has been visited
by different people at different times.
The location of the place is imprecise.
Perhaps it is a point between this and that,
or perhaps it is a little further to the south.

* * *

El cuerpo del agua está metido
entre muros verduzcos, musgosos,
se llena y se vacía según las mareas que
el río vierte en el océano
o que el océano empuja en la boca del río.
Al borde de un receptáculo que podríamos llamar piscina
nos sentamos
y miramos hojas rojizas y marrones
caídas desde los árboles de la ribera,
agujas de pino
algas
aletas,
el chapoteo negro del hombre sumergido.

En la mano de goma del buceador: unas gafas de sol
                              un carrete de fotos
                              una libreta.

* * *

The mass of water is enclosed
between green, mossy walls,
is replenished and empties according to the tides which
the river pours into the ocean
or which the ocean pushes into the mouth of the river.
At the edge of a receptacle that we could call a swimming pool
we sit down
and we look at reddish and brown leaves
fallen from the trees on the bank,
pine needles
algae
fins
the black splashing of the submerged man.

In the diver's rubber hand: a pair of sunglasses
                              a roll of film
                              a notebook.

* * *

En sueños mato a uno,
no sé a quién.
No recuerdo el hecho, ni la
sucesión de los actos,
pero tengo la conciencia del crimen.
El temporal empuja desde el puerto
a quien regresa a
los ojos rasgados y licuosos
de la casa.
Leo en la libreta los movimientos
que describe la que persigue al
actor que ensaya el monólogo.
Creo leer la soledad del barco de
hocico oxidado en su misión de
ir y venir. También la
soledad del actor, la del personaje,
y la de la mujer que toma notas.
No me muevo de la casa.

* * *

In dreams I kill someone,
I do not know whom.
I do not remember the deed, nor the
succession of actions,
but I am conscious of the crime.
The storm surges from the quay
towards the person returning to
the almond-shaped and watery eyes
of the house.
I read in the notebook the movements
described by the woman pursuing the
actor who is rehearsing the monologue.
I believe I can read the loneliness of the boat with
the rusted prow in its mission of
coming and going. Also the
loneliness of the actor, that of the character,
and that of the woman who is taking notes.
I do not leave the house.

* * *

Petirrojo de cuerpo diminuto, de un solo ojo abierto.
Lo trae la gata hasta el cuarto de baño
lo veo tendido como un despojo. Muerto, y sin embargo, bello.
El poeta explicaba el poema como un artefacto hecho de
                             despojos, trozos, tropiezos
no digeridos que sobresalen en el vómito. Con los trozos que el
                                                 estómago
no ha triturado, que los ácidos no han corroído, ni los líquidos disuelto,
hago el poema. Así, el texto se vuelve sólido y el poema es
lo que se traga sin ser masticado.
Lo que aprieta en el estómago.
Si creyera en esas cosas, pensaría que con su ofrenda la gata
me recuerda que soy mortal.
¿Lo habrá matado ella? ¿Cayó de frío? ¿Sufrió al morir?
Diciembre, ese mes tan extraño.
Hay años que llueve mucho y río abajo se oye el agua como el
                                         galopar de los caballos.
No esta noche. Este diciembre huele a sangre y a hojarasca,
y así suena el filo metálico de la luna que guía a la transeúnte
hasta la casa fría, donde el gato le quita el abrigo,
le besa en la frente, le da de comer.

* * *

A robin with a tiny body, with only one eye open.
The cat brings it as far as the bathroom
I see it laid out like a spoil. Dead, and beautiful.
The poet would explain the poem as an artefact made from the
                              leftovers, pieces, undigested
chunks which protrude in vomit. With the pieces which the stomach
has not dissolved, which the acids have not corroded, nor the liquids
                                            broken down,
I make the poem. In this way the text is solid and the poem is
what is swallowed without being chewed.
That which tightens the stomach.
If I believed in these things, I would think that with her offering the cat
was reminding me that I am mortal.
Did she kill it? Did it die of cold? Did it suffer at the end?
December, this month so strange.
There are years when it rains a lot and down river the water sounds
                                        like the galloping of horses.
Not tonight. This December smells of blood and fallen leaves,
and that is what the metal blade of the moon sounds like, guiding
the passer-by towards the cold house, where the cat takes off her coat,
kisses her on the forehead, gives her something to eat.

PADRE

Los brazos, blandos por la natación, no me dejan escribir.
Los oídos se me van detrás de la niña que toca el piano
a las órdenes del padre que entona.
Lo hacen tan mal que podría poner un disco,
pero me flaquean las piernas.
Anoto el sueño del padre
que enseña a follar. En otro sueño hay una mujer
que enseña, pero no es la madre. A él pensaba
que lo había matado.
Ella no sé quién es.

FATHER

The arms, soft from swimming, do not let me write.
The ears elude me behind the girl who plays the piano
on the orders of the father who is singing.
They are doing so badly that I could put on a record,
but I am too tired to move my legs.
I note the dream of the father
who is giving her a lesson in fucking. In another dream there is a woman
who is teaching, but it is not the mother. I thought
I had killed him.
I do not know who she is.

MADRE
My mother makes me sick but I love her.
                                        Anne Sexton

Visitarla me despeja.
Cultivo cosas como el cariño y la armonía.
Una vez quise escribir como si fuera ella
en un mundo gris, animal, represor.
Llegué tan adentro que tuve que
dejarlo.
Fue como volver al útero y
encarnarme en la embarazada,
encaramarme en la mirada adolescente
de las fotos que me mostró.

MOTHER
My mother makes me sick but I love her.
                                        Anne Sexton

Visiting her clears my head.
I cultivate things such as love and harmony.
Once I wanted to write as if I were her
in a grey, bestial, oppressive world.
I went so far inside it that I had to
leave.
It was like returning to the womb and
taking the role of a pregnant woman,
looking through her adolescent eyes
in the photographs that she showed me.

YO

Me dice que jamás se autorretrató
aunque veo algunas fotos suyas que imitan la técnica del
fotomatón. Otras en las que juega con cierta ambigüedad:
gabardina, sombrero, silla,
con la escenografía de quien quiere acompañarse.
Notas de diario.
La escritura crece a la vez que las imágenes fotográficas
con el pelo y las uñas
las plantas
los dedos de sarmiento de los geranios
que cada otoño hay que cortar,
como se corta lo que se va escribiendo
de una hoja a otra,
o se rompen fotos:
nariz en un pedazo, labios en otro.
El estruendo interrumpe la frase.
Surgen la fractura, el quiebro
en continua crisis
el dedo que oprime el disparador,
los que sujetan la pluma
captura rapaz
entre lo hecho y el desecho.

ME

She tells me that she never took her own portrait
although I see some photos of her that imitate the technique of the
photo booth. There are others in which she plays with a certain ambiguity:
gabardine, hat, chair,
with the stage set of someone who wants to provide her own company.
Entries in a diary.
Writing grows at the same time as the photographic images
with the hair and the nails
the plants
vinelike fingers of the geraniums
which have to be cut back each autumn,
as you cut back what you are writing
from one page to the other,
or you tear up photos:
nose in one piece, lips in another.
The thunder interrupts the phrase.
They emerge, the fracture, the swaying movement
in continuous crisis
the finger that releases the shutter,
those that hold the pen
predatory capture
between the fact and the waste.

* * *

Me coloco detrás de él
que sobresale entre los edificios de la plaza
irregular, desordenada.
Bruno murió en una hoguera
que para él prepararon aquí
el 17 de febrero de 1600.
Dos personas tocadas como él con capuchas
pero de colores
cruzan el campo que ahora es el de las flores
de largos tallos envueltos en celofán
el de la lechuga mojada
el de las pisadas que esparcen rojo y semillas de tomate,
el campo de la bicicleta negra apoyada en el pedestal.

* * *

I stand behind him
as he rises up among the buildings of the piazza,
which is uneven, untidy.
Bruno was burned at the stake
in a fire they prepared for him here
on 17 February 1600.
Two people wearing hoods like him
albeit coloured ones
cross the square where flowers are now sold
with broad stalks wrapped in cellophane
where you can find the wet lettuce
where footsteps scatter redness and tomato seeds,
the square with the black bicycle leaning against the pedestal.

* * *

Nada ocurre tal y como ocurre en el poema.
Tampoco en la fotografía
que sólo dice: yo estuve allí.
Ocurre algo singular y efímero:
arco iris en el pelo alborotado de la ola
remolino de agua alrededor de pies que se hunden en la arena
cuerpo negro sobre tabla.
Precipitación extemporánea
signos negros sobre hoja blanca y rayada.

* * *

Nothing happens in the way that it happens in the poem.
It is the same in the photograph
which only says: I was there.
Something extraordinary and ephemeral happens:
a rainbow in the dishevelled hair of the wave
a whirlpool around the feet which are sinking in the sand
black body on a surfboard.
Untimely precipitation
black signs on the white and ruled page.

* * *
*Como cuando una persona ha entrado tan profundamente en un sueño
que jamás recordará que estuvo allí una vez de vuelta en su habitación.*
                              Tomas Tranströmer

La noche pasa como una enfermedad no superada por el día.
La palabra golpea la cama y es
el perro que se abalanza sobre ella
que camina y sin temblar se detiene
y lo mira. En otro sueño él
la ha tirado al suelo, etc.
Se reconocen en el recuerdo de sangre
que se forma entre sus ojos
como un charco
desde cuyo fondo sólo se ven la espalda de ella y los talones
que empujan hacia abajo.
El perro es cercano como un hombre
y de igual complexión atlética.
De la cama se evapora la palabra del sueño
que enturbia la mañana.

* * *

As when a man goes so deep into his dream he will never remember that he was there when he returns again to his room.
                                    Tomas Tranströmer

The night passes like an illness not overcome by the day.
The word strikes the bed and it is
the dog which rushes on to the woman
who is walking and without shivering she stops
and looks at it. In another dream he
has pulled her to the ground, etc.
They recognise each other in recalling the blood
which forms between their eyes
like a pool
from the depths of which you can only see her shoulder and the heels
which push downwards.
The dog is close like a man
and of an equally athletic complexion.
From the bed there evaporates the word of the dream
which is clouding the morning.

* * *
Vuelta al sueño desde la habitación

La cama es un pozo
un cilindro musgoso de paredes verdes
por el que caigo con la vista clavada
en la lámpara
cada vez más lejana.
La cama ya no me sostiene.
Pierdo el recuerdo de lo que es
y alcanzo una manera movediza
de estar en este lugar de
ausencia intermitente.
La mujer interrumpe su conversación
y me mira desde el otro lado de
una mesa larga donde se amontonan
piezas brillantes de cubertería.
"Es un amor sin objeto" dice.
Me asustan sus manos enguantadas
el paño ennegrecido con
el que me va borrando la cara.

*　*　*
Return to the dream from the room

The bed is a well
a mossy cylinder with green walls
down which I fall staring
at the lamp
which is further and further away.
Already the bed cannot hold me.
I forget what it is
and reach a restless way
of being in this place of
intermittent absence.
The woman interrupts her conversation
and looks at me from the other side of
a wide table on which gleaming
pieces of cutlery are piling up.
"It is a love without object" she says.
Her gloved hands startle me
the blackened cloth with
which she is rubbing out my face.

* * *

La máquina de museo consigue detener el agua,
la contiene. Cesa el rumor de las turbinas.
El pez se encona en una esquina de la pecera.
No abre la boca. Presiona con la cabeza
el vértice del cristal desde la cola
con movimientos que sacuden el seno del agua
como un látigo.
La superficie apenas se inmuta.
El pez es oscuro, de bordes irisados.
Los dedos de ella arden. Se los chupa. Aspira.
De las uñas brota sangre negra y traza
signos sobre una libreta. Luego, la mano
se queda atrapada entre las hojas de un libro.
Hay un hombre con barba
que se inclina sobre mí
acerca la mejilla a la cara transparente del acuario
y habla mi idioma.

* * *

The engine from the museum manages to stop the water,
contains it. The noise from the turbines stops.
The enraged fish swims into the glass in a corner of the fish tank.
It does not open its mouth. It presses with its head
against the side of the tank making movements
with its tail that whip up the water
from within.
The surface is hardly disturbed.
The fish is dark, its outline iridescent.
Her fingers burn. She sucks them. She breathes.
Black blood flows from her nails and leaves
signs on a notebook. Later, her hand
remains trapped between the pages of a book.
A man with a beard
leans over me
brings his cheek close to the transparent face of the aquarium
and speaks my language.

* * *
> *¿Acaso no sabías que la puerta era estrecha?*
> Rafael Cadenas

Hay un sobresalto inesperado pero regular
cada vez que se sumerge
y olvida las coordenadas de su situación.
Saberse lejos – en mitad de –
contrae los pasillos estrechos
por los que debería pasar el oxígeno.
No ve
si en el fondo
alguien sostiene una espada o
un estetoscopio.
El paso es estrecho.
Toma aire y vuelve a sumergirse.
Inalterable, impasible
el miedo
sigue intacto.

* * *
> *Perhaps you did not know that the doorway was narrow?*
> Rafael Cadenas

She has an unexpected but regular fright
every time she dives
and forgets the co-ordinates of her situation.
Being far away – in the middle of –
she contracts the narrow passageways
through which the oxygen has to pass.
She does not see
if on the bottom
someone is holding a sword or
a stethoscope.
The passage is narrow.
She draws breath and dives again.
Unalterable, impassive
the fear
remains intact.

* * *

El viento debe de ser eso:
una bolsa de lluvia arrastrada
bultos de niebla y agua
que pasan por lentes y ventanas
a gran velocidad.
La mujer del hospital no ha muerto aún
y él sigue en el autobús
conversando con la rubia que fuma.
Llevo horas dormida en
un atasco permanente y definitivo.
En el sueño
alguien trata de demostrar que
el viento tiene cuerpo, y dice
no sé qué de las almas furiosas de los muertos
muertos por rencor.
La luz sigue roja.

* * *

The wind must be this:
a carrier of drawn up rain
pockets of fog and water
that pass through lenses and windows
at high speed.
The woman from the hospital has not yet died
and he is still on the bus
talking to the blonde who smokes.
I spend hours asleep in
a permanent and definitive traffic jam.
In the dream
someone tries to show that
the wind has substance, and says
something about the furious souls of the dead
who died of rancour.
The light is still red.

***

Paso las hojas de la libreta.
Hay alguna foto.
Algunos ya no están. Ella sí, pero
en las páginas todos viven al mismo nivel.
Como en la enciclopedia, todas las fotografías son del mismo tamaño.
Lleva meses trabajando
pero el sueño se repite:
quiere pagar, su dinero no sirve;
llega a la frontera, no es ella la mujer del pasaporte;
olvida los guantes en un vagón, vuelve por ellos,
no regresa.
Le sale un extraño círculo en el hombro
un círculo irregular, de trazo tembloroso
como si repentinamente al lápiz se le hubiera roto la punta.
Sangra. Al teléfono
la mujer le da las gracias por el libro del médico.

* * *

I turn the pages of the notebook.
There are some photos.
Some are not there. She is, but
on the page everyone is of equal importance.
As in the encyclopedia, all the photographs are of the same size.
She spends months working
but the dream recurs:
she wants to pay, her money is not accepted;
she arrives at the frontier, she is not the woman in her passport;
she forgets her gloves in a train carriage, goes back for them,
does not return.
A strange circle appears on her shoulder
an irregular circle, unsteadily drawn
as if suddenly the sharpened tip of the pencil had broken.
She bleeds. On the telephone
the woman thanks her for the doctor's book.

* * *

Me cortan un trozo de carne del hombro.
Ante el espejo
no respondo.
La voz no sale
la garganta se llena de piedras
gravilla
granos de arena
grumos
espinas.
Hay algo áspero en los dedos
al pasar las hojas,
miniaturas
visiones exprimidas
hebras que brillan y borran
caminos falsos
versiones de lugares equivocados.
El ritmo de la máquina es espeso.
La luz pasa lenta.
La mujer posa con pereza.
El hombro le tapa el cuello
los párpados ocultan los ojos
la nariz, con su sombra, le corta
la barbilla.
Está la inclinación de la cabeza,
la de las palas de la máquina
la pendiente.

* * *

They cut a piece of skin from my shoulder.
Before the mirror
I do not reply.
There is no voice
the throat fills with stones
gravel
grains of sand
lumps
bones.
There is something harsh in the fingers
when turning the pages
miniatures
visions extracted like a juice
threads which shine and erase
wrong paths
versions of mistaken places.
The rhythm of the machine is sluggish.
The light passes slowly.
The woman poses lazily.
The shoulder covers up the neck
the eyelids conceal the eyes
the nose, with its shadow, cuts off
her chin.
There is the inclination of the head,
that of the blades of the engine
the slope.

* * *

Los cuerpos se tienden sobre
gomas infladas,
las gomas negras se mecen sobre
el agua,
las primeras aguas se filtran al
piso de abajo, al
suelo, al subsuelo, se
escurren pedazos de conversación,
música, palabras sueltas.
Las gomas están enganchadas con
cadenas, se aflojan o
se tensan al ritmo de la marea que
impulsa el pulmón.
La luz sigue encendida.
La máquina sacude las olas, las sábanas.
No hay agua más estancada que
la de mis ojos
cada vez más rojos.

* * *

The bodies lie down on
inflated tyres,
the black tyres rock on
the water,
the water at the bottom leaks into
the flat below, into
the ground, into the subsoil,
scraps of conversation slip away,
music, individual words.
The tyres are attached with
chains, they drift apart or
are pulled taut by the tide's rhythm which
the lung quickens.
The light is still on.
The engine shakes the waves, the sheets.
There is no water more stagnant than
that of my eyes
which become redder and redder.

* * *

El viento de la máquina bate
las hojas de la palmera.
Hay un gato que trepa por el delgado tronco
y se detiene sin llegar al enjambre de
palmas secas.
La palmera es una señora flaca y descolorida
con la cara alargada,
calada con un sombrero de espadas verdes.
El gato es un mono que quiere besarla
y se pierde en el paisaje borroso de su peinado.
No es una selva, es el patio inundado de una ciudad con
pies que evitan el agua, brazos
que no consiguen detener la máquina.
Estoy en la laguna enmarañada de sus ojos,
en la orilla de los libros,
en los agujeros del número.

* * *

The wind from the machine strikes
the leaves of the palm tree.
There is a cat who is climbing up the narrow trunk
which stops without reaching the cluster of
dry palm leaves.
The palm tree is a thin and faded woman
with an elongated face,
wearing a hat with green swords.
The cat is a monkey who wants to kiss her
and gets lost in the blurred landscape of her coiffure.
It is not a jungle, it is the flooded courtyard of the city with
feet which avoid the water, arms
which do not manage to stop the machine.
I am in the tangled pool of her eyes,
on the shore of the books,
in the holes of the figure.

BIOGRAPHICAL NOTES

ELI TOLARETXIPI was born, lives and works in San Sebastian, Spain. She has published two poetry collections in Spanish and her poetry has also been translated into French and Italian. *Amor muerto naturaleza muerta* (Past Love Still Life) was published in 1999 and was praised for its poetics of unease. Her second volume *Los lazos del número* (The Loops of the Figure) appeared in 2003. Structurally dazzling, its poems deal with perception, dream and the nature of poetry. She is the Spanish translator of Elizabeth Bishop, Sylvia Plath, Menna Elfyn and Tess Gallagher.

PHILIP JENKINS translates contemporary Spanish poetry and lives in Spain. He and R. D. V. Glasgow have translated *The Black Sheep and Other Fables* (Acorn Book Company, 2005) by the Guatemalan writer Augusto Monterroso.

ROBERT CRAWFORD has published six collections of poetry, four of which have been Poetry Book Society Recommendations; he has also won two Scottish Arts Council Book Awards. With Simon Armitage he edited *The Penguin Book of Poetry from Britain and Ireland since 1945* (1998) and with Mick Imlah *The New Penguin Book of Scottish Verse* (2000).

A founding editor of the magazine *Verse*, he has served as a judge for the T. S. Eliot Prize, the National Poetry Competition, and other awards. He has been Professor of Modern Scottish Literature at the University of St. Andrews since 1989.

Also available in the Arc Publications
'VISIBLE POETS' series
(Series Editor: Jean Boase-Beier)

No. 1
MIKLÓS RADNÓTI (Hungary)
Camp Notebook
TRANSLATED BY FRANCIS JONES
INTRODUCTION BY GEORGE SZIRTES

No. 2
BARTOLO CATTAFI (Italy)
Anthracite
TRANSLATED BY BRIAN COLE
INTRODUCTION BY PETER DALE
(Poetry Book Society Recommended Translation)

No. 3
MICHAEL STRUNGE (Denmark)
A Virgin from a Chilly Decade
TRANSLATED BY BENTE ELSWORTH
INTRODUCTION BY JOHN FLETCHER

No. 4
TADEUSZ RÓŻEWICZ (Poland)
recycling
TRANSLATED BY BARBARA BOGOCZEK (PLEBANEK) & TONY HOWARD
INTRODUCTION BY ADAM CZERNIAWSKI

No. 5
CLAUDE DE BURINE (France)
Words Have Frozen Over
TRANSLATED BY MARTIN SORRELL
INTRODUCTION BY SUSAN WICKS

No. 6
CEVAT ÇAPAN (Turkey)
Where Are You, Susie Petschek?
TRANSLATED BY CEVAT ÇAPAN & MICHAEL HULSE
INTRODUCTION BY A. S. BYATT

No. 7
JEAN CASSOU (France)
33 Sonnets of the Resistance
WITH AN ORIGINAL INTRODUCTION BY LOUIS ARAGON
TRANSLATED BY TIMOTHY ADÈS
INTRODUCTION BY ALISTAIR ELLIOT

No. 8
ARJEN DUINKER (Holland)
The Sublime Song of a Maybe
TRANSLATED BY WILLEM GROENEWEGEN
INTRODUCTION BY JEFFREY WAINWRIGHT

No. 9
MILA HAUGOVÁ (Slovakia)
Scent of the Unseen
TRANSLATED BY JAMES & VIERA SUTHERLAND-SMITH
INTRODUCTION BY FIONA SAMPSON

No. 10
ERNST MEISTER (Germany)
Between Nothing and Nothing
TRANSLATED BY JEAN BOASE-BEIER
INTRODUCTION BY JOHN HARTLEY WILLIAMS

No. 11
YANNIS KONDOS (Greece)
Absurd Athlete
TRANSLATED BY DAVID CONNOLLY
INTRODUCTION BY DAVID CONSTANTINE

No. 12
BEJAN MATUR (Turkey)
In the Temple of a Patient God
TRANSLATED BY RUTH CHRISTIE
INTRODUCTION BY MAUREEN FREELY

No. 13
GABRIEL FERRATER (Catalonia / Spain)
Women and Days
Translated by Arthur Terry
Introduction by Seamus Heaney

No. 14
INNA LISNIANSKAYA (Russia)
Far from Sodom
Translated by Daniel Weissbort
Introduction by Elaine Feinstein

No. 15
SABINE LANGE (Germany)
The Fishermen Sleep
Translated by Jenny Williams
Introduction by Mary O'Donnell

No. 16
TAKAHASHI MUTSUO (Japan)
We of Zipangu
Translated by James Kirkup & Tamaki Makoto
Introduction by Glyn Pursglove

No. 17
JURIS KRONBERGS (Latvia)
Wolf One-Eye
Translated by Mara Rozitis
Introduction by Jaan Kaplinski

No. 18
REMCO CAMPERT (Holland)
I Dreamed in the Cities at Night
Translated by Donald Gardner
Introduction by Paul Vincent

No. 19
DOROTHEA ROSA HERLIANY (Indonesia)
Kill the Radio
TRANSLATED BY HARRY AVELING
INTRODUCTION BY LINDA FRANCE

No. 20
SOLEIMAN ADEL GUÉMAR (Algeria)
State of Emergency
TRANSLATED BY TOM CHEESMAN & JOHN GOODBY
INTRODUCTION BY LISA APPIGNANESI